About the au

Steve Biddle is a professional entertainer and Origami expert. He has been teaching Origami to children and adults since 1976. While he was in Japan studying under the top Japanese Origami Masters, he met and married his wife Megumi. Megumi is one of the foremost Japanese paper artists working in *Washi* hand-made Japanese paper, and her work has received many top awards in Japan and abroad. She has designed for some of Japan's top fashion designers, and has worked on many award-winning commercials for Japanese television. Since their return to England, Steve and Megumi have taken their craft all over the country to schools, festivals and arts centres, and have designed for television and feature films. They present Origami as entertainment, art and education to young and old alike.

*Also available in Beaver
by Steve and Megumi Biddle*

Things to make in the Holidays

NEWSPAPER MAGIC

Steve and Megumi Biddle

Illustrated by Megumi Biddle

Beaver Books

A Beaver Book
Published by Arrow Books Limited
62–5 Chandos Place, London WC2N 4NW

An imprint of Century Hutchinson Ltd

London Melbourne Sydney Auckland
Johannesburg and agencies throughout the world

First published 1989

Set in Times
by JH Graphics Ltd, Reading

Made and printed in Great Britain
by Anchor Brendon Limited
Tiptree, Essex

ISBN 0 09 961010 8

Contents

Introduction

The newspaper is a very useful (and cheap) item that can be folded, rolled or torn to make many decorative, entertaining and magical objects.

With newspaper magic, presentation is very important, so try to remember the following things when you give a show with some of the magical newspaper items found in this book.

Your show should have:

- a very good unexpected opening
- a few entertaining tricks in the middle
- and a very good trick to end with.

Always try to build a story to tell around each item that you show. It does not matter how silly the story is, as long as it is entertaining and fits your personality.

Be careful what page of newspaper you use for any newspaper trick. Let the headlines tell happy news or news that is unimportant — your trick and the audience might be affected if you use a page of newspaper that tells bad news.

When folding your newspaper, always pick a hard, flat surface, like the top of a table, to fold upon. Be very careful to make your folds straight, and make them sharp by pressing along them with your thumb.

Always start with a new or nearly new newspaper, as it will make the finished item look a lot better than if you were to use a very old and dirty newspaper.

But above all, please never tell anyone how a newspaper trick is done. KEEP THE SECRET TO YOURSELF!

We hope you have a great deal of fun and enjoyment with *Newspaper Magic!*

Steve and Megumi

Acknowledgements

We would like to thank Lillian Oppenheimer, Tomomi Kudo, Toshie Takahama and our many friends in the Nippon Origami Association for sharing their ideas with us.

Paper Sizes

Sheet: Many of the items to be found in *Newspaper Magic* start with a sheet of newspaper taken from a large-sized newspaper. This is a full-page spread, consisting of two pages with a fold down the middle.

Large square: For many of the origami hats and a few of the other items we need to have a large square of newspaper. So here is a quick and easy way to make one.

You will need: *a sheet of newspaper*
scissors

1 Fold the sheet of newspaper in half from right to left along its middle fold.

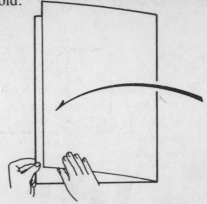

2 With the folded edge on your right-hand side, fold the paper in half from bottom to top.

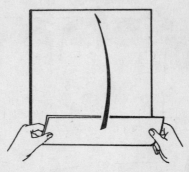

3 Fold the right-hand side edges over to meet the bottom folded edge, so making a triangle.

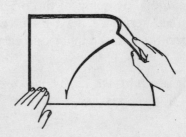

4 Cut along the left-hand side edge of the triangle, and discard the rectangular shape of paper.

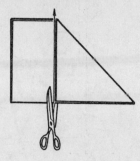

5 Open out the triangle to make your square. You will see many fold-lines in the square that will be useful later on.

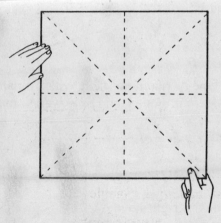

Page: Quite a few of the other items to be found in *Newspaper Magic* start with a page of newspaper taken from a large-sized newspaper. This is half a sheet which has been either cut or torn in half along the middle fold.

Small square: One or two items start with a small square of newspaper. Here is a quick and easy way to make one.

You will need: *a page of newspaper*
scissors

1 Fold the bottom right-hand edge over to meet the left-hand side, so making a triangle.

2 Cut along the top edge of the triangle, and discard the rectangular shape of paper.

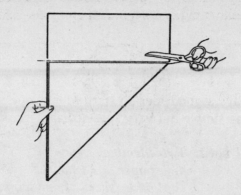

3 Open out the triangle to make your square.

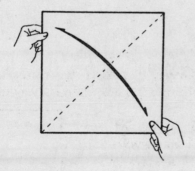

Magic Tricks

Magic words

It is always a good idea to start your magic show with something simple but very spectacular. Here's one idea.

You will need: *Two identical sheets of newspaper — A and A'*
One other sheet of newspaper — B
Glue
Black felt-tip pen

1 Place sheet B flat on a table. Glue sheet A on to the left side of sheet B.

2 Glue sheet A′ on to the right side of sheet B.

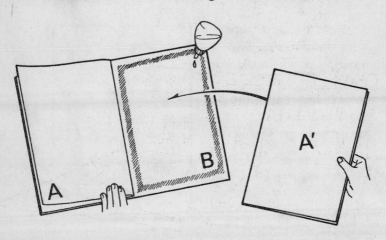

3 Glue sheets A and A' together, so making a flap that can be moved from side to side.

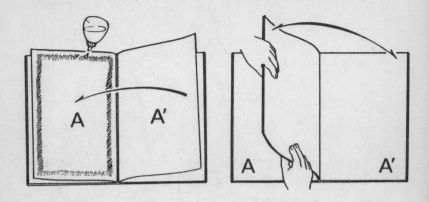

4 On side A', write the words NEWSPAPER MAGIC with the black felt-tip pen.

5 Hold the newspaper with the movable flap hanging downwards, so making the newspaper look blank, and hiding the words NEWSPAPER MAGIC.

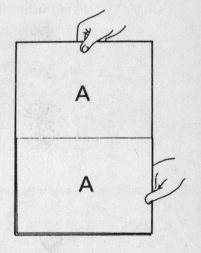

6 Fold up both the bottom edges (as one) to meet the top edge.

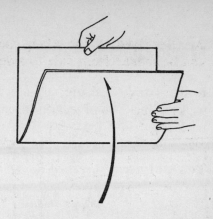

7 Say the magic word 'Abracadabra', and let go *only* of the front thickness of newspaper . . .

8 to produce your magic words!

You could write many other words on to sheet A', for example, HAPPY BIRTHDAY or MERRY CHRISTMAS.

Magic cone

In the world of magic, a magician uses many different tricks to make an object disappear. Here is a very simple trick for you to try.

You will need: *sheet of newspaper*
glue
paper tissue

Before you start, place the sheet of newspaper flat on a table.

1 On the right side of the sheet glue *only* along the shaded lines.

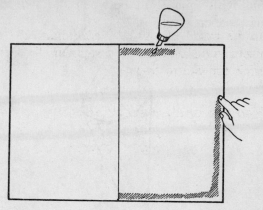

2 Fold the left side of the newspaper over to meet the right side, along the middle fold, so gluing them together.

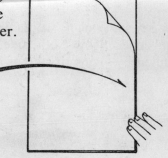

3 Roll the newspaper up into a cone, making sure that the unglued open edges are at the top.

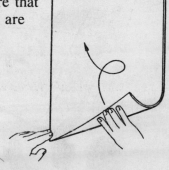

4 Pretend to put the paper tissue into the magic cone, but really put it in between the two open layers of newspaper.

5 Say some magic words like 'Hey Presto' and flick open the cone. Show both sides of the newspaper to the audience — your tissue has vanished!

6 To make the tissue reappear, roll the newspaper up again into a cone, making sure the unglued open edges are at the top. Say a few magic words.

7 Carefully reach down inside the two open layers of newspaper and, to the amazement of your audience, pull out the paper tissue.

With the magic cone you can also vanish and produce other small items, like string, ribbon and confetti.

It's in the news

One of the most popular magic tricks for a magician to perform is to produce from out of nowhere a beautiful silk handkerchief. As silk handkerchiefs are very hard to find, we shall use instead a colourful paper tissue.

You will need: *sheet of newspaper*
colourful paper tissue
glue

Before you start, place the sheet of newspaper flat on a table.

1 Place the tissue on the left side of the paper, in the centre. Glue the paper *only* along the shaded lines, taking great care *not* to glue the tissue to the newspaper.

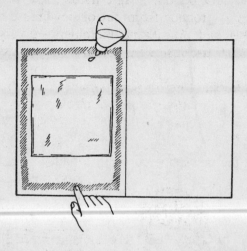

2 Fold the right side of paper over to meet the left side, along the middle fold, so gluing the two sides together with the tissue inside.

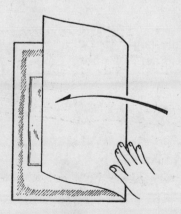

3 Show both sides of the newspaper to the audience.

4 Screw the newspaper up into a ball.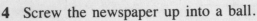

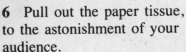 **5** Say a magic word like 'Sim Sala Bim!', and tear the surface of the newspaper.

6 Pull out the paper tissue, to the astonishment of your audience.

If, at the start of the trick, you pack about six or seven paper tissues inside the newspaper, you will then be able to perform a very colourful illusion.

Torn and restored newspaper

This magic effect is a classic in the world of magic. You tear a newspaper into many small pieces, say a few magic words, and then magically restore them into the original piece of newspaper.

You will need: *two identical pages of newspaper — A and B*
glue

1 Lay page A sideways on a table. Put a little glue (about the size of a postage stamp) on the top left-hand corner of page A. Place page B exactly on top of page A and glue the two top left-hand corners together.

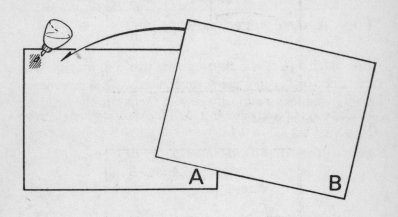

2 Now fold *only* page B in half from right to left.

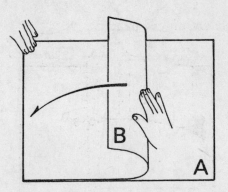

3 Fold page B in half again from right to left.

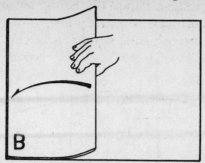

4 Once again fold page B in half from right to left. Press the paper flat.

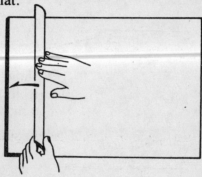

5 Completely unfold page B.

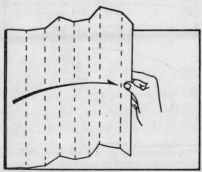

6 · Now fold page B backwards and forwards along the fold-lines, (you may have to reverse some of the fold-lines) so pleating it into a concertina-like strip.

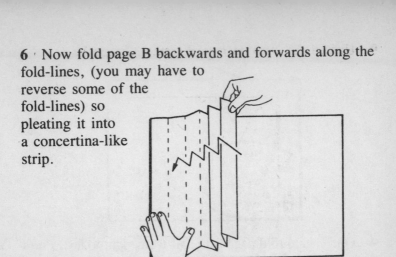

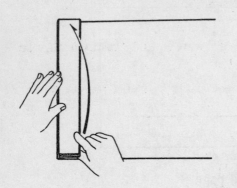

7 Fold the pleated strip in half from bottom to top.

8 Fold it in half again from bottom to top. Press the paper flat.

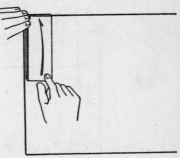

9 Unfold the strip back to the start of step 7.

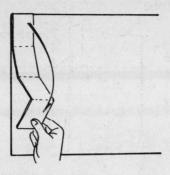

10 Pleat the strip forwards and backwards, so making . . .

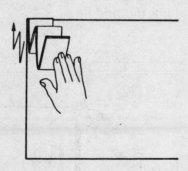

11 a neatly folded package in the top left-hand corner.

You are now ready to perform the famous Torn and Restored Newspaper trick.

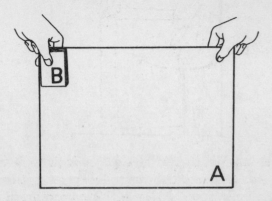

12 With the folded package facing you, hold the newspaper in your left hand with your left thumb over the folded package. Using your right hand, hold and tear page A in half along the middle.

13 Place the torn, right-hand piece of paper behind the left-hand piece.

14 Once again tear the newspaper in half along the middle. As before place the right-hand pieces behind the left-hand pieces, still keeping the folded package B under your left thumb.

15 Turn the paper sideways and tear in half again along the middle. Place the right-hand pieces behind the

left-hand pieces, always
keeping the folded package B
under your left thumb.

16 Repeat step 15 one
more time.

17 This is your view of the paper — which you must
be very careful *not* to show to the audience.

18 Say a magic word or two. In doing so, turn the torn
pieces of newspaper over, so that package B is now

behind them. Take hold of the top corner of package B, and pull it slowly out of your hand, so that it unfolds. Take great care to hide the torn-up pieces of paper in your left hand, so that nobody will see them. Now you are . . .

19 performing the famous Torn and Restored Newspaper trick! Try it again. Remember that in magic, practice makes perfect.

Invisible thread

Megumi learnt this trick from a friend during her childhood in Japan.

You will need: *strip of newspaper about 18cm × 4cm*
scissors

1 Place the strip of newspaper on a table. Fold it in half from bottom to top. Press the strip flat along the fold-line and then unfold it.

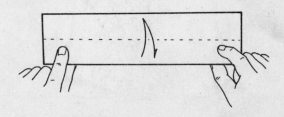

2 From the right-hand side, make a cut along the middle fold, about 4cm long.

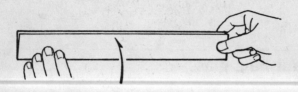

3 Now fold the strip back in half again from bottom to top.

4 Hold the cut end between your right thumb and forefinger. Move your thumb and forefinger and the paper will move from side to side. Pretend to tie an invisible thread to the paper.

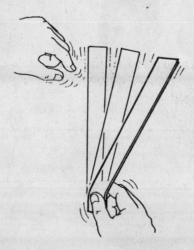

5 Move your left hand steadily backwards and forwards, at the same time secretly moving your right thumb and forefinger, so convincing your audience that the invisible thread is moving the paper.

Vanishing glass

This is another classic from the world of magic. It is a big favourite with Steve, as he likes to perform it when we have guests for dinner.

You will need: *clear glass or plastic tumbler*
two pages of newspaper

1 Sit at a table and place a glass and two pages of newspaper in front of you.

2 Pick up the two pages of newspaper together, as if they were one piece.

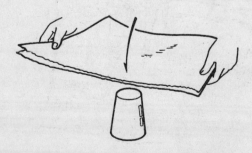

3 Wrap the pages of newspaper around the glass. Make sure that the shape of the glass can be seen very clearly.

4 Start to move the glass and newspaper in circles around the table.

5 Bring the glass towards you across the table. Without looking at the glass and newspaper, secretly let the glass drop from underneath the paper into your lap, being careful not to let it drop to the floor.

6 Place the paper glass shape back on the table. As the paper will still hold the shape of the glass, no one will think that the glass is no longer there.

7 With your hand crush the paper down flat on to the table top.

8 To the amazement of your audience, the glass will have vanished! Pretend that the glass passed through the table by reaching under the table to retrieve it (whilst really picking it up from your lap). Place it back on the table.

A fishy tale

This is a fun piece of magic that also has a story. You are trying to find your pet cat, so you wrap up a picture of a fish as bait. Then you say a few magic words. Upon unwrapping the picture, you find a picture of your grinning cat, along with the skeleton of the fish that he has eaten.

You will need: *two identical pages of newspaper*
glue
piece of card
ruler
scissors
felt-tip pens

1 Take one of the pages of newspaper and fold over the left side one-third.

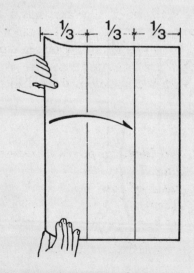

2 Fold over the right side to lie exactly on top of the left side.

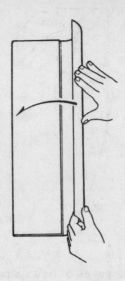

3 Fold up the bottom edges one-third.

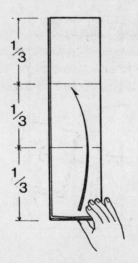

4 Fold down the top edges to lie exactly on top.

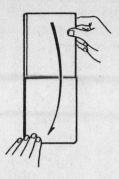

5 This is package A.

6 Fold the other page of newspaper in exactly the same way as package A, making sure that this package (package B) has exactly the same news stories on the outside as package A. Glue packages A and B together, back to back.

7 Completely unfold package B. From the piece of card draw and cut out two 'postcards' that are slightly smaller than the centre rectangle of package B. With the felt-tip pens, draw a picture of a grinning cat along with the skeleton of a fish on one of the postcards. Place this picture into the centre of package B. Now fold up package B in exactly the same way . . .

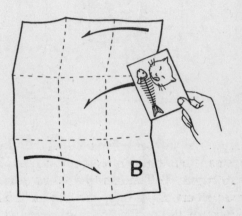

8 as before. Turn the packages over, so that package A is now on top.

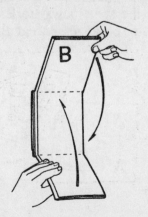

9 Completely open out package A.

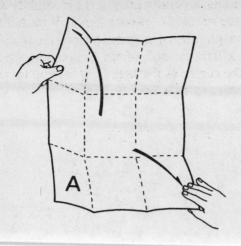

10 Draw a picture of a fish on the other postcard. Place this postcard into the centre of package A. You are now ready to begin. Tell the story of how you are trying to find your pet cat. So as bait, you will use a fish. You show the picture of the fish to the audience and start to . . .

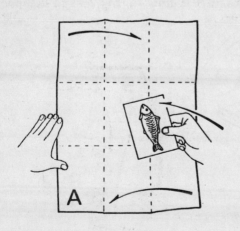

11 fold up package A (with the fish picture inside) in exactly the same way as package B.

12 Once package A is folded, pick up both the packages as one from the table. Be very careful not to let the audience see package B. Say a few magic words. Put the packages back on the table. In doing so turn them over, so that package B is now on top.

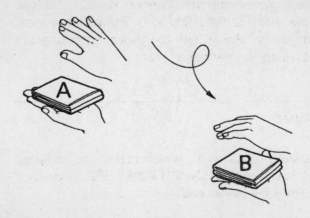

13 Say a few more magic words about your cat. Unfold package B and, to the surprise of your audience, you will have found your pet cat, who has also eaten the fish!

The important part of this trick is telling the story, because by doing this you take the attention of the audience away from what you are doing with the paper, so they won't spot you turning the packages over.

Magic tube

This is called a spoof trick, which means the audience thinks they have found out how it works. But, as always, the magician wins in the end.

You will need: *page of newspaper*
two paper clips
ball of string
scissors

1 Lay the page of newspaper in front of you on a table.
Fold it in half from left to right.

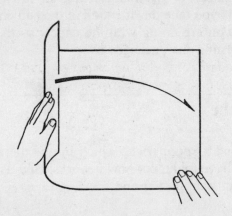

2 Fold it in half again from left to right.

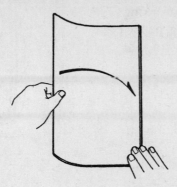

3 Start to roll the paper into a tube from the bottom edges.

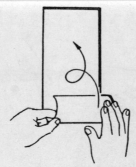

4 When you have rolled the paper up, hold the tube in place with the help of one paper clip.

5 Cut two lengths of string, each about 1m long. Double over each piece of string. Fix the remaining paper clip to one piece of string, at its centre.

6 Fasten this paper clip to the tube, at the opposite end to the first paper clip. Pass the other doubled length of string through the tube, from the end of the first paper clip.

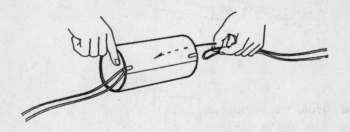

7 Thread one set of doubled strings through the other set . . .

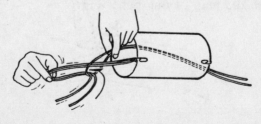

8 so that they look
like this.

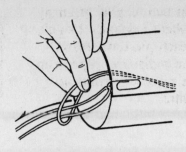

9 Pull the strings back inside the tube, so that it now
looks as if a double string is running through the tube.

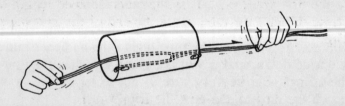

10 Hold the strings and
the tube in this position.

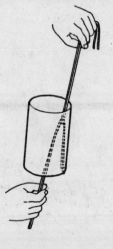

11 By pulling the bottom strings, the tube will appear to climb up the string. To make the tube climb down, simply hold the top strings, relax the bottom strings, give a little shake, move your hands together a little, and the tube will come down.

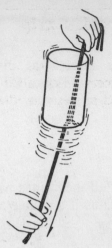

12 To make the spoof work on the audience, this is what you do. As you pass the tube out to the audience, turn it upside-down, and it will not climb up when they pull the strings. But be very careful not to let anyone look inside the tube to see how the trick works.

Moebius strip

This effect was discovered by an astronomer and mathematician called Augustus Ferdinand Moebius, who lived in Germany during the last century.

You will need: *page of newspaper*
scissors
ruler
felt-tip pen
glue

1 Cut three long strips of paper from the page of newspaper, each about 5cm wide.

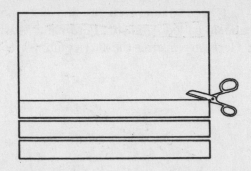

2 Label the strips *a*, *b*, and *c*.

3 Take strip *a* and glue the ends together, so making a loop.

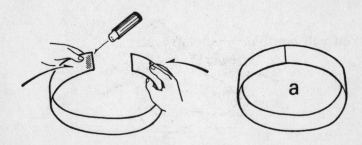

4 With strip *b*, give it half a turn (180 degrees) before gluing the ends together to make a loop.

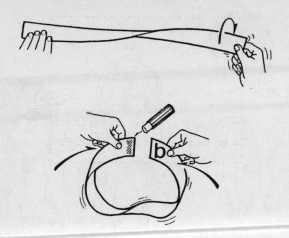

5 Last of all give strip *c* a full turn (360 degrees) before gluing the ends together to make a loop.

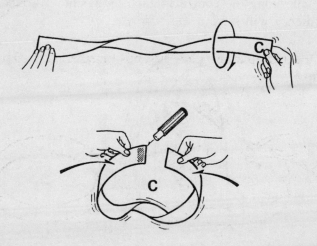

6 Now give loops *b* and *c* to members of the audience. Even though all the loops look the same, if you . . .

7 cut along the centre of each loop, both you and the audience will have a big surprise.

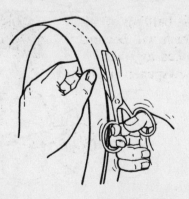

8 Loop *a* will become two separate loops of paper.

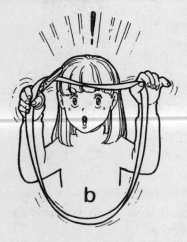

9 Loop *b* will become a single loop that is double the size of the original loop.

10 The most baffling of all is loop *c*, which will become two loops linked together. Now that's newspaper magic for you!

Water and confetti

It is always nice to close a performance of newspaper magic with a colourful and spectacular finale. Water and confetti is another trick that Megumi learned during her childhood days in Japan.

You will need: *two sheets of newspaper*
two small clear plastic bags
box of confetti
sticky tape
glue
glass of water (about half-full)

1 Open out one sheet of newspaper flat on a table. Fill one of the plastic bags about one-third full with confetti.

Fasten the plastic bags to the newspaper with small pieces of sticky tape on either side of the middle fold.

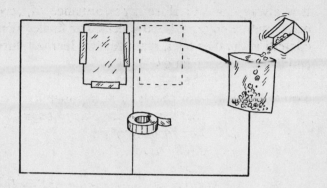

2 Place glue on the paper along the shaded lines, but do *not* glue along the top of the plastic bags. Place the second sheet of newspaper on top, so gluing the two sheets together.

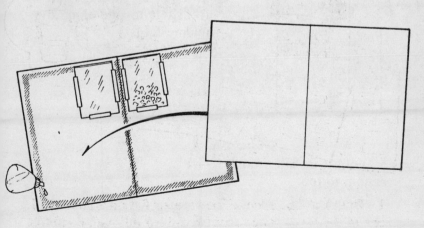

3 Hold the newspapers between your hands with the opening at the top.

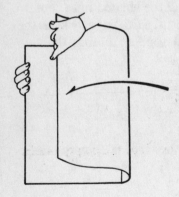

4 Fold the paper in half from side to side along the middle fold.

5 Fold it in half from bottom to top.

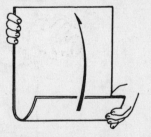

6 Fold it in half again from side to side.

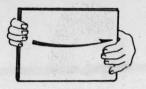

7 Push your forefinger into the paper where the empty plastic bag is. Move your forefinger around to open the top of the bag.

8 Carefully pour the glass of water into the empty plastic bag.

9 Then open out the newspaper . . . .

10 and the water will appear to have vanished!

11 Fold up the newspaper as before and pour the water back into the glass. Make sure no confetti falls out.

12 Push your forefinger into the paper where the confetti is. Move your forefinger around to open the top of the bag, and say a few magic words.

13 Hold the paper upside-down and swing it from side to side, so that the confetti flies out, making a beautiful finale to a show of newspaper magic.

Puzzles and other fun items

Walking through a newspaper

This puzzle is so old that many people have forgotten all about it. The question to ask your friends is: How can you walk through a page of newspaper?

You will need: *page of newspaper*
scissors

1 Place the page of newspaper flat on a table. Fold it in half from bottom to top.

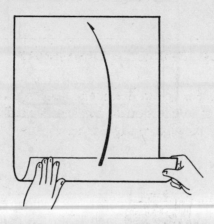

2 From the folded edge make two cuts towards the opposite edges, as shown. Be careful *not* to cut right through to the opposite edges of the newspaper.

3 Cut away a section of paper 2cm wide from between the two cuts.

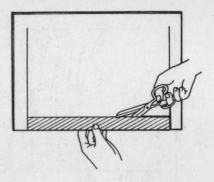

4 Now cut slits in the paper, each about 2cm apart, first from the top edge and then from the bottom edge. As before, be very careful *not* to cut right through to the opposite edges of the newspaper.

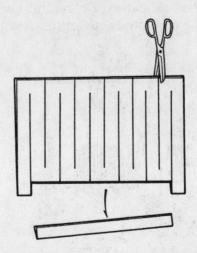

5 From the bottom edge, pick up two sections of the top sheet. Gently pull the paper out from the middle, until you have made . . .

6 a loop of newspaper, which is big enough for you to walk through!

Circle — square

Watch out for a surprise ending, because with this puzzle things are not always what they seem!

You will need: *page of newspaper*
scissors
glue

1 From the page of newspaper, cut two short strips of paper each about 5cm wide.

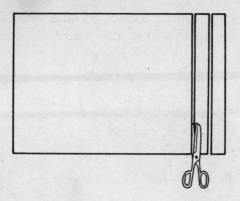

2 Take each strip in turn and glue the ends together, so making . . .

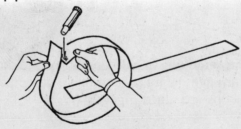

3 two separate loops.

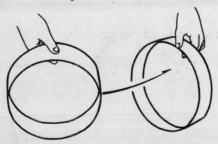

4 Glue one loop inside the other as shown . . .

5 so that they look like this.

6 Cut the outer loop in half lengthways. Make sure you only cut through the inner loop once, at the point where the two loops are glued together.

7 Nearly there . . .

8 You should now have two loops joined together by a strip. Cut this strip in half lengthways, to produce the surprise ending . . .

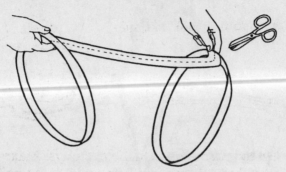

9 a square!

Bat and ball

When we were on holiday in New York City, we came across this quick and very easy way to make a bat and ball.

You will need: *four sheets of newspaper*
sticky tape

Before you start, cut or tear along the middle fold-lines of each sheet, to make eight pages.

1 Place six of the pages on top of each other. From one short side roll them together into a tight tube.

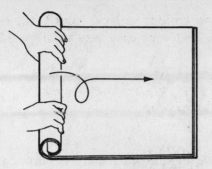

2 Fasten the tube together with strips of sticky tape, to stop it unrolling.

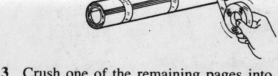

3 Crush one of the remaining pages into a ball.

4 Wrap sticky tape all around the ball to make it firm and tight.

5 Wrap the last page of newspaper around the ball. As before, make the ball firm and tight by wrapping sticky tape around it.

6 Why not have a game of bat and ball outside with your friends? The instructions for making a paper baseball hat and glove follow next.

Baseball hat

When we were both living in Tokyo, in Japan, we visited a school to see what children were learning about origami or paper folding. During the course of our visit, some of the children taught us how to fold this baseball hat.

You will need: *square made from a sheet of newspaper*

1 Put the square of newspaper on a table with one corner facing you, so it looks like a diamond. Fold the top corner down to meet the bottom corner.

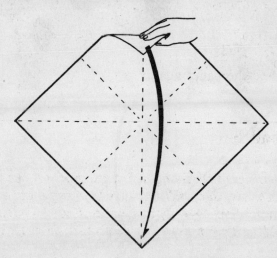

2 Fold up the bottom corners to meet the top folded edge, but do *not* press the paper completely flat.

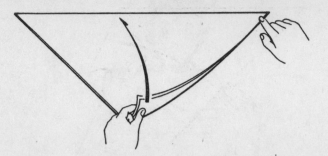

3 Press the paper only a little, at this bottom point.

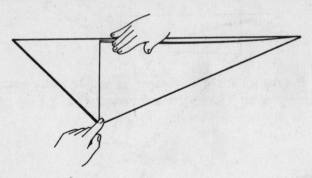

4 Unfold the paper again.

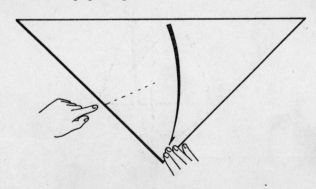

5 Fold the right-hand point down to meet the fold mark that you made in step 3.

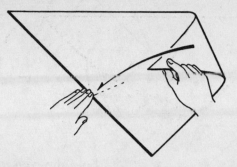

6 Fold the left-hand point over to touch the opposite side.

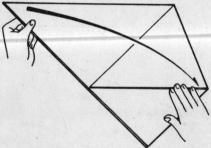

7 Fold up the top layer of the bottom corner, as far as it will fold. This corner will become the peak of your hat.

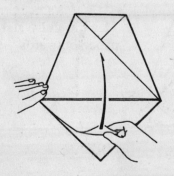

8 Tuck the other bottom corner inside the hat.

9 Fold the peak down a little.

10 Turn the hat sideways.

11 Carefully start to pull the paper outwards . . .

12 to make your hat. As you
do so, push the top of the
hat in.

13 Press the paper flat.
Hold the peak and . . .

14 pull it upwards,
pressing it into place,
to make . . .

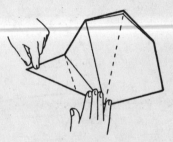

15 your baseball hat.

Baseball glove

It was on a cold winter's day, while we were staying with
our niece Tomomi, that some of her school friends taught
us how to fold this baseball glove.

You will need: *sheet of newspaper*

Keep the sheet of newspaper folded in half along its
middle fold-line.

1 With the folded edge of the newspaper on your right-hand side, fold the newspaper in half from right to left. Press flat and unfold.

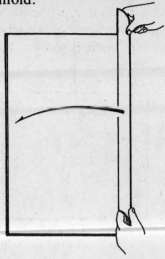

2 Fold in the two top corners, so that they lie on the middle fold-line.

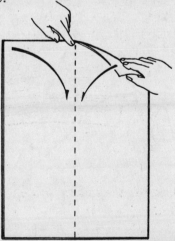

3 Fold over the right folded edge, so that it lies along the middle fold-line.

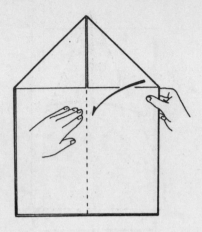

4 Fold over the left folded edge in the same way.

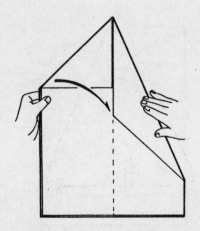

5 Your paper should now look like this. Turn the paper over from side to side.

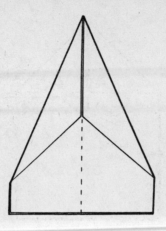

6 Fold the bottom edges over and over, about three times, to make a band of paper about 4–5cm wide.

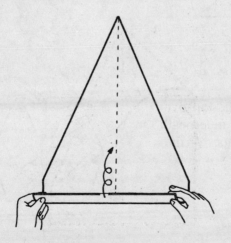

7 Fold in the ends of the band, so that they touch the middle fold-line.

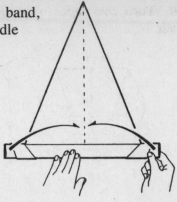

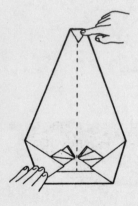

8 Fold the top point down a little.

9 Bend the top over, tucking it underneath the band of paper at the bottom.

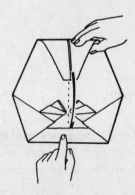

10 Turn the paper over from side to side to make your . . .

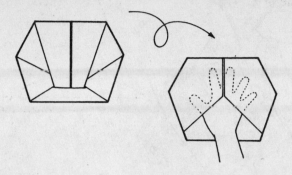

11 baseball glove.

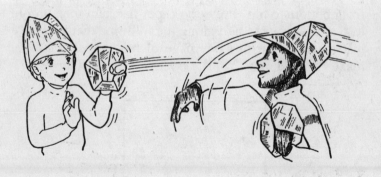

Snapper

One of our friends showed us how to make this very noisy snapper when we were teaching at a summertime fun workshop in our local art centre.

You will need: *page of newspaper scissors*

1 Place the page of newspaper on a table. Fold it in half from bottom to top. Press the paper flat, and then unfold it. Cut the paper in half along the fold-line that you have just made. From this one page of newspaper, you can make two snappers.

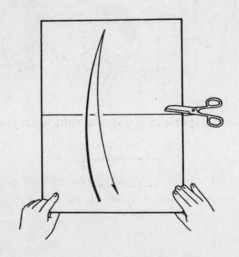

2 Taking one half-page, fold it in half from left to right.

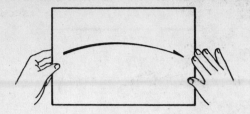

3 Fold the paper in half from bottom to top.

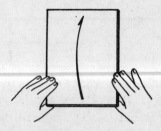

4 Again fold the newspaper in half from bottom to top.

5 Press the paper flat along the fold with your thumb.

6 Once again, fold the newspaper in half from bottom to top. Press the paper flat and then unfold it.

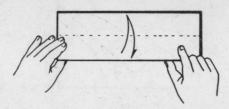

7 Cut a slit along the fold-line from the right-hand edge to the middle.

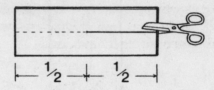

8 Fold both the top and bottom edges to the middle fold-line, pressing the paper flat as you do so.

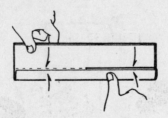

9 Fold the newspaper in half from bottom to top.

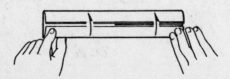

1 Fold the rectangle of newspaper in half from bottom to top, and then unfold it.

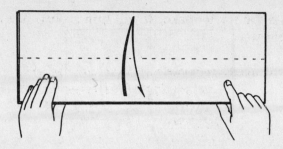

2 Make three cuts in the paper as shown, being careful to cut only one-third of the distance.

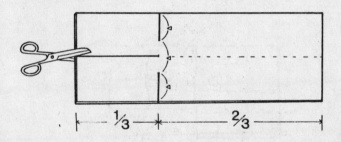

3 Fold the right side over to meet the cuts.

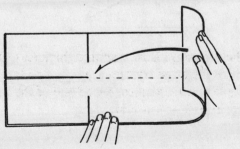

4 Fold up the bottom right-hand edges as far as the cut will allow you.

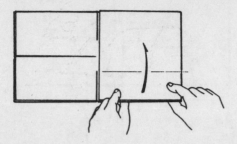

5 Fold down the top right-hand edges, again as far as the cut will allow you.

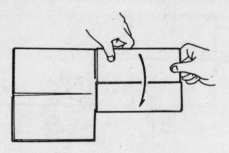

6 Fasten the edges together with a piece of sticky tape.

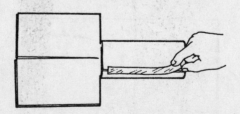

7 Bend over the unfolded edges to make the helicopter blades, giving them a soft curve.

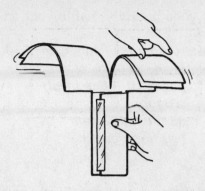

8 Drop the helicopter from a height and watch it whirl around and around.

The impossible puzzle

This is a very good puzzle to baffle your friends with.

You will need: *rectangle of newspaper (the one cut in the making of the large square on pages 10–11 is ideal)*
scissors
needle and cotton
two large buttons

Because the rectangle is of a double thickness (due to the way we make the large square), separate one layer, so that you now have two rectangles. Place one of the rectangles, still folded in half, on a table. Cut this rectangle in half along the middle fold line, so from this one rectangle of newspaper you can make two Impossible puzzles.

1 Fold the rectangle of newspaper in half from bottom to top.

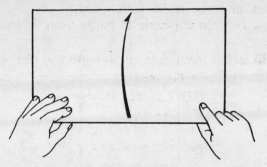

2 Cut a little slot in one end of the paper as shown. Then unfold the rectangle.

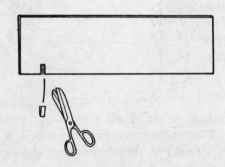

3 Fold the rectangle in half from left to right.

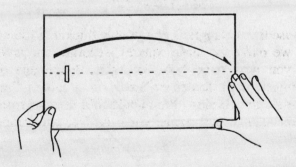

4 From the folded side, make two parallel cuts that go towards, but do not quite touch the slot. Make sure you cut them the same width as the slot.

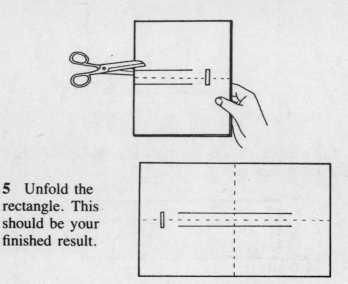

5 Unfold the rectangle. This should be your finished result.

6 Now bend the ends of the newspaper towards each other, but not quite together. Thread the strip made by the two parallel cuts in step 4, through the slot, so that you get a little loop sticking out.

7 Thread the buttons on to a length of cotton and knot the ends so the buttons don't fall off.

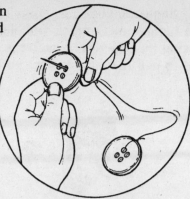

8 Put one of the buttons through the loop.

9 Fold the paper back into place so that it looks like this.

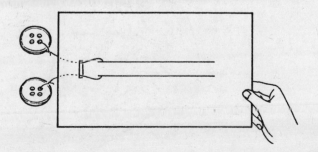

10 Show the puzzle to your friends. Ask them if they can remove the buttons without breaking the cotton or tearing the paper. The secret is simply to repeat step 6 and to pull the buttons back through the loop.

Necktie

Our niece Tomomi showed us how to make this necktie and the fish that follows. She learned how to make both items at school.

You will need: *rectangle of paper (the one cut in the making of the large square on pages 10–11 is ideal)*
scissors

Because the rectangle is of a double thickness (due to the way we make the large square), separate one layer, so that you now have two rectangles. Place one of the rectangles, still folded in half, on a table. The other rectangle can be used to make the fish (see page 105).

1 Fold the rectangle in half from bottom to top.

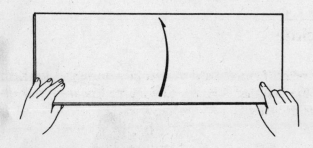

2 Fold it in half a second time from bottom to top.

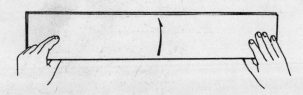

3 Unfold. Cut along one of the quarter fold lines to produce a strip of paper, still folded in two.

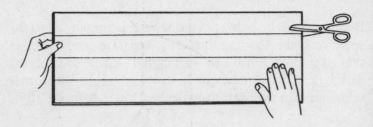

4 Open out the strip of paper. Turn it so it is lengthways on to you.

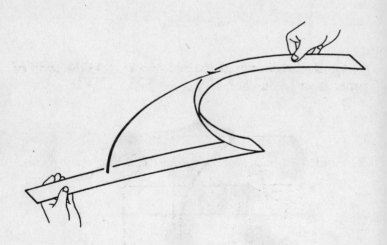

5 On the lower side of the centre line, fold the top half of the strip of paper over to the left in a 45 degree fold.

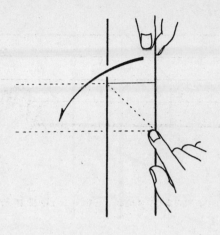

6 On the other side of the centre line, fold the strip of paper over in another 45 degree fold.

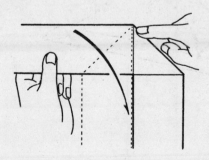

7 Now start to weave the strips. Fold this strip forwards to the right in another 45 degree fold and tuck it underneath the other strip.

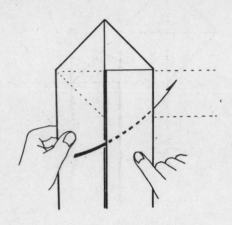

8 Then fold it backwards.

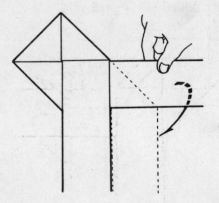

9 Once again fold the left-hand strip forwards to the right and tuck it underneath the other strip.

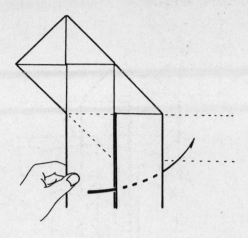

10 As before, fold this strip backwards. Carry on folding until the necktie is long enough.

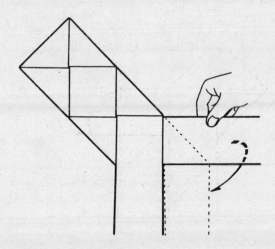

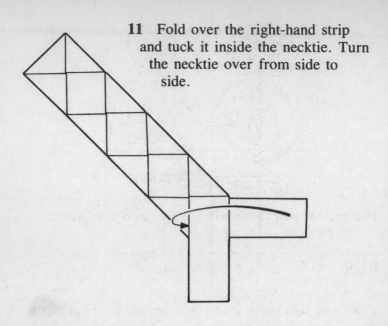

11 Fold over the right-hand strip and tuck it inside the necktie. Turn the necktie over from side to side.

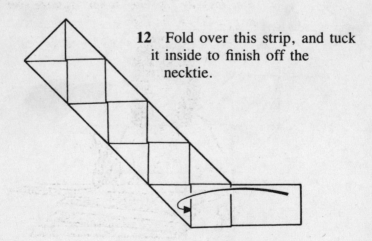

12 Fold over this strip, and tuck it inside to finish off the necktie.

The necktie will also make a very good bookmark.

Fish

This fish could make a very nice mobile for your room.

You will need: *rectangle of paper (the one cut in the making of the large square on pages 10–11 is ideal)*
scissors
cotton

To help you when you are making the fish, try to keep the paper in the same place on the table during the folding. Don't keep turning it around and around.

Before you start, prepare your paper by following steps 1, 2 and 3 of the Necktie on pages 99–100. Then cut along each of the fold-lines to make four strips of paper (each one folded in two) A, B, C and D.

1 Take strips A and B and put A inside B like this.

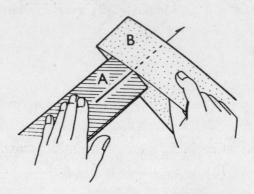

2 Weave strip C into place.

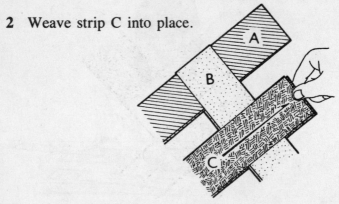

3 Carefully weave strip D into place.

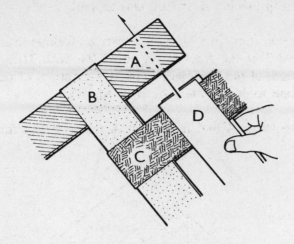

4 Pull the strips in the directions shown to make a paper knot.

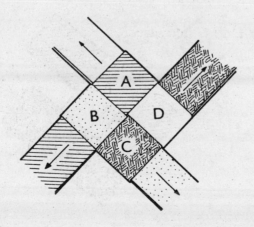

5 Fold the top layer of strip B up over the knot.

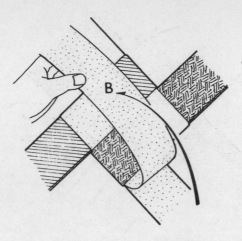

6 Fold the top layer of strip A up over the knot.

7 Now fold the top layer of strip D over the knot.

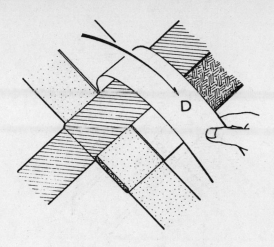

8 Fold the top layer of strip C over the knot, taking great care to weave it through.

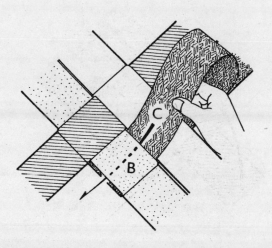

9 Your paper should now look like this.

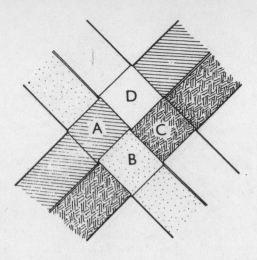

10 In turn, fold over the bottom layers of strips A and D and weave them through.

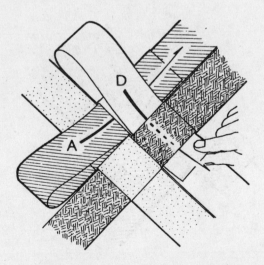

11 Pull the strips tight. Turn the paper over from top to bottom.

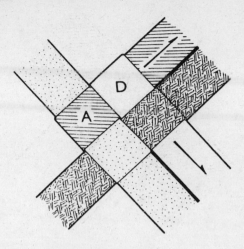

12 Fold over the bottom layers of strips B and C and weave them through. Turn the paper over from top to bottom.

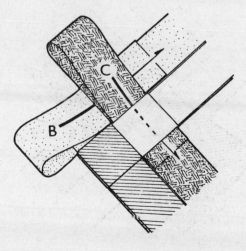

13 Fold the top layer of strip A backwards.

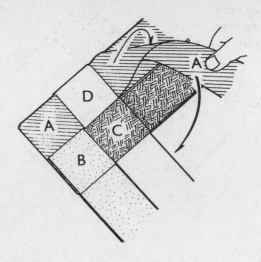

14 Fold the top layer of strip B backwards.

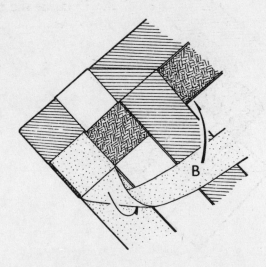

15 Trim each of the strips to the same length, being very careful not to trim. them too short.

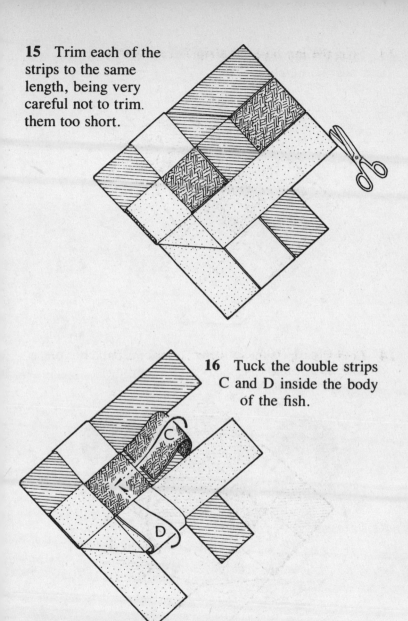

16 Tuck the double strips C and D inside the body of the fish.

17 Cut off the remaining ends as shown to suggest tail and fins, so making . . .

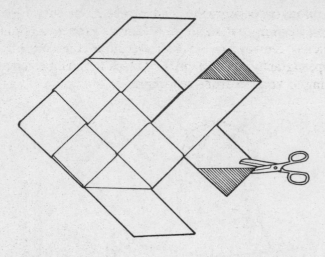

18 your fish. To make it into a mobile, attach a piece of cotton to it and hang it from the ceiling.

Chapeaugraphy

The word chapeaugraphy is an eighteenth-century French word meaning 'hat-writing'. A famous French magician, Felicien Trewey, in the 1870s made a complete act of chapeaugraphy, using a circle of black felt. You can make a simple version from newspaper.

You will need: *large square made from a sheet of newspaper*
scissors
ruler

1 Fold the square in half from left to right.

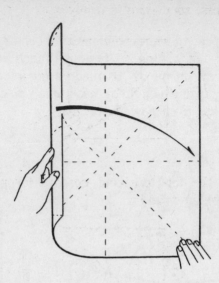

2 Fold it in half again from bottom to top.

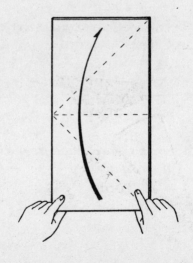

3 Fold the bottom right-hand corner up to meet the top left-hand corners, so making a triangle.

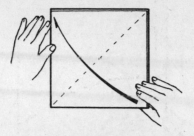

4 Fold over the top left-hand corners to meet the opposite side of the triangle.

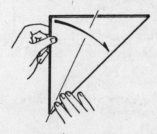

5 Measure and cut off the shaded parts, taking great care to cut a curve each time.

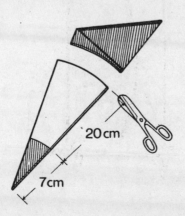

20 cm

7 cm

6 Open out the newspaper to produce your chapeaugraphy ring.

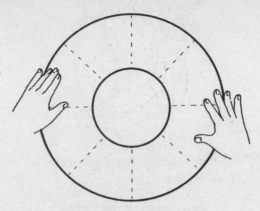

7 By twisting, folding and curling the ring you can make many different hats. Here are just a few for you to try.

8 Sun hat

9 Fashion hat

10 Cowboy hat

11 Napoleon hat

12 Pirate hat

Why not try to invent a few of your own?

Paper Tearing

Paper tearing was very popular in the music hall acts of Victorian and Edwardian times. Today, if you are very lucky, you can sometimes watch paper tearing being performed on a television variety show or at a theatre.

Tree

This is an easy item to make by paper tearing. If you find that tearing the paper is too hard for your fingers, you can cut out the designs with a pair of scissors.

You will need: *two sheets of newspaper*
scissors
glue
sticky tape

1 Open out the two sheets of newspaper and place them flat on top of each other. Fold the bottom edges up to meet the top edges.

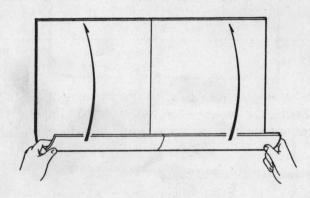

2 Press the paper flat with your thumb.

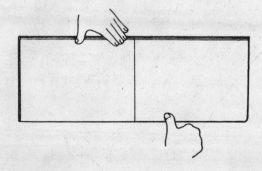

3 Unfold the newspaper. Cut through all the layers of the newspaper along the *long* fold-lines, making four rectangles of newspaper.

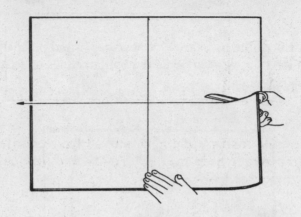

4 Roll one rectangle of newspaper loosely into a tube.

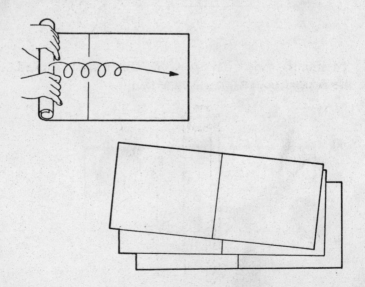

5 Before you reach the end, glue on another rectangle of newspaper.

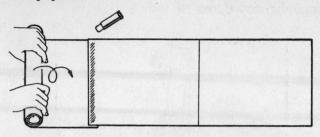

6 Keep on rolling and gluing until all the rectangles of newspaper have been used up. You should now have a paper tube that looks like this.

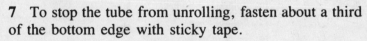

7 To stop the tube from unrolling, fasten about a third of the bottom edge with sticky tape.

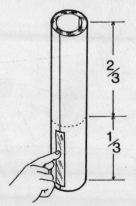

8 From the top of the tube make four vertical cuts, cutting through all the layers of paper, to a point about two-thirds of the way down the tube.

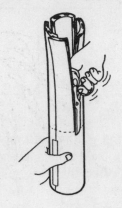

9 Bend the cut pieces downwards.

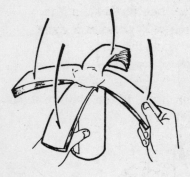

10 Hold the top inside centre layer and start . . .

11 to pull out the centre layers of paper, making sure as you do so, that you are holding the bottom of the tube tightly.

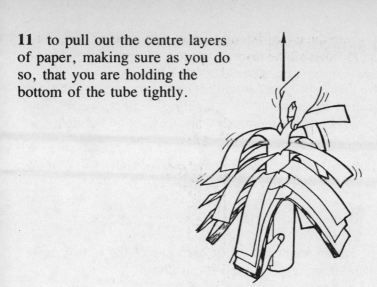

12 As you pull the centre layer further and further out, the tree will grow in a most magical way.

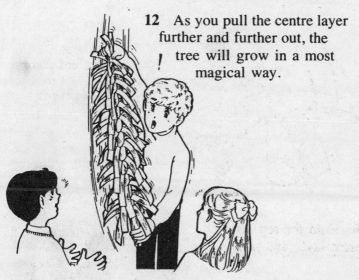

For a more colourful tree, try using the comic pages of a newspaper.

Ladder

No display of paper tearing is complete without the paper ladder. Even though it is a very old effect, we still find that an audience is amazed when they see one being made.

You will need: *roll of paper (repeat steps 1 to 6 of the Tree on pages 121–3)*
sticky tape
scissors

1 Fasten about a third of each end of the roll of paper with sticky tape, to stop it unrolling.

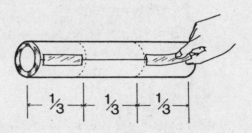

2 Remove the middle third of the roll, by cutting through all the thicknesses of paper as shown.

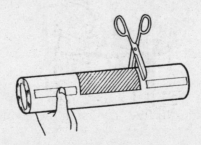

3 Bend down the two ends of the roll as shown.

4 Hold each end tightly.

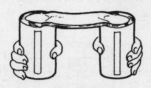

5 Then, with the help of a friend, carefully pull up the top layer of paper.

6 Gradually pull each layer of paper, until you have . . .

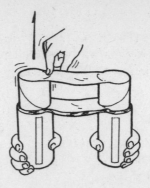

7 stretched the ladder to its full height.

The ladder will stand up by itself if placed against the edge of a table, or the back of a chair.

Paper chain

Here is a fun way to make a very simple Christmas decoration. We were shown how to make this by a very kind and dear friend, Toshie Takahama, who lives in Tokyo, Japan.

You will need: *roll of paper (repeat steps 1 to 6 of the Tree on pages 121−3)*
sticky tape
scissors

1   Fasten sticky tape along the edge of the tube, to stop it unrolling. Cut the tube in half.

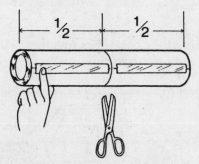

2   Make another cut in the middle of one of the sections. The cut should go almost through the tube, but be very careful *not* to cut all the way through.

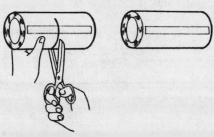

3 Bend the tube backwards in half, where you have cut it.

4 It should now look like this.

5 Carefully hold the two tubes together. Put your finger and thumb inside the two tubes.

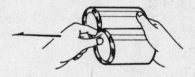

6 With your finger and thumb, start to pull out the inside layers of paper and a . . .

7 paper chain will grow from the inside of the cut roll.

Try using several sheets of coloured newspaper to make a much more stunning paper chain.

Snowflakes

Using this simple, traditional Japanese kirigami or paper cutting technique you can make a beautiful snowflake.

You will need: *page of newspaper scissors*

1 Fold the page of newspaper in half from bottom to top.

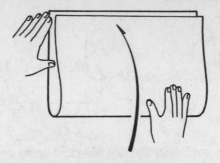

2 Fold it in half from right to left.

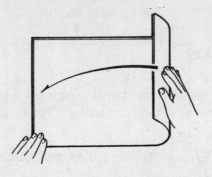

3 Press the paper flat and unfold it.

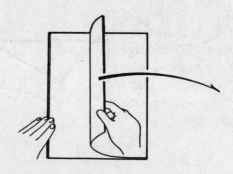

4 Fold the left-hand side edges in to meet the fold-line. Press the paper flat and unfold.

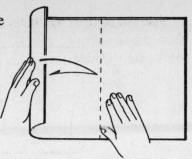

5 Carefully fold over the bottom right-hand corner, from the middle of the bottom folded edge, so that it touches the foldline in step 4.

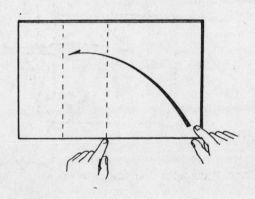

6 Again from the middle of the bottom folded edge, fold over the bottom left-hand corner, so that it lies along the sloping edge of the right side.

133

7 The folding may not be exact, but this does not matter. Turn the newspaper over from side to side.

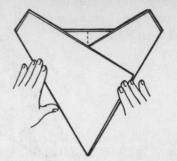

8 Fold the paper in half from left to right along the middle fold-line.

9 Press the paper flat.

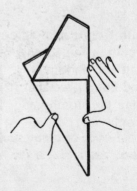

10 Cut away the shaded parts with the scissors.

11 Carefully open out the paper to make a most wonderful snowflake.

This is only one of many such shapes that you can make. See if you can make a few more of your own.

Five-pointed star

This is a very easy way to make a lovely star, with just a few simple folds and one cut of the scissors.

You will need: *page of newspaper*
scissors

1 Lay the page of newspaper flat on a table. Fold it in half from bottom to top.

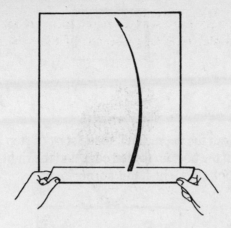

2 Fold it in half from right to left.

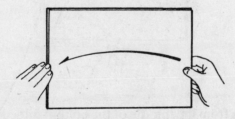

3 Fold it in half from bottom to top.

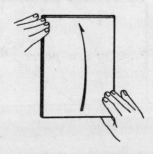

4 With your thumb press the paper flat.

5 Open out the paper back to the start of step 2. From the middles of the bottom folded edge and the right-hand edge, fold the bottom right-hand corner over.

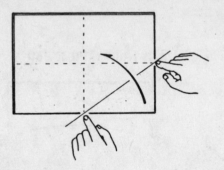

6 Again from the middle of the bottom folded edge, fold over the right-hand side.

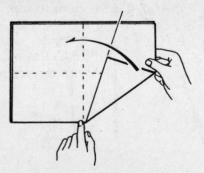

7 For the last time, fold over the right-hand side from the middle of the bottom folded edge.

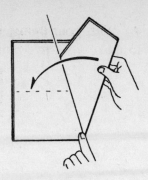

8 Fold over the bottom left-hand corner, so that it lies along the sloping edge of the right-hand side, and press the paper flat. The folding may not be exact but this does not matter.

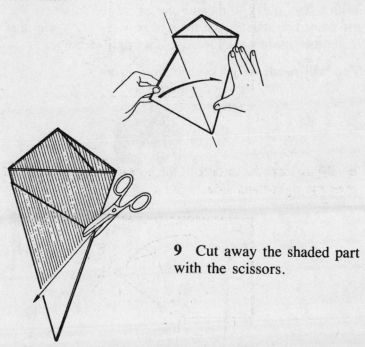

9 Cut away the shaded part with the scissors.

10 Open out the small triangle to make your five-pointed star.

Knockout

With a few, quick folds and one cut of the scissors, you can make five stars in one sheet of newspaper. Again, this is another traditional Japanese kirigami technique.

You will need: *large square made from a sheet of newspaper*
scissors

1 Fold the square in half from top to bottom.

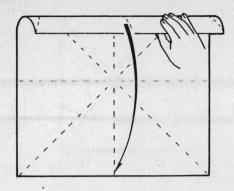

2 Fold it in half from left to right.

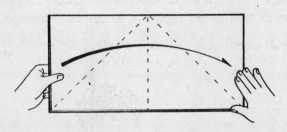

3 Fold the top left-hand corner down to meet the bottom right-hand corners.

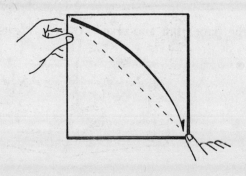

4 Fold the top bottom right-hand corner up to meet the middle of the diagonal slope.

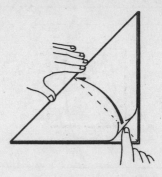

5 Fold both the top right-hand and bottom left-hand corners over to meet the bottom right-hand corners.

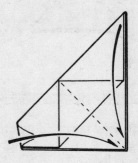

6 Press the paper flat and turn it over.

7 Fold the paper in half, from the top right-hand corner to the bottom left-hand corner, along the diagonal fold-line, so making . . .

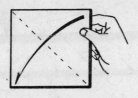

8 a triangle.

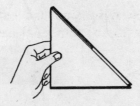

9 With the scissors carefully cut away the shaded part.

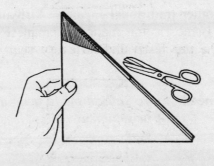

10 Open the paper out carefully and you should have a knockout result!

Paper net

This is another traditional Japanese kirigami item. The paper net is most often made by Japanese children for *Tanabata*, a star festival, held every year on 7 July.

You will need: *large square made from a sheet of newspaper*
scissors

1 Lay the square flat on a table, and fold it in half from bottom to top.

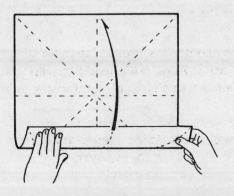

2 Fold it in half from left to right.

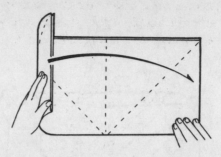

3 Fold the bottom right-hand corners up to meet the top left-hand corner, so making a . . .

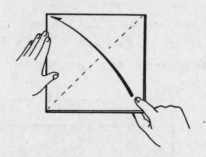

4 triangle. Press the paper flat with your thumb.

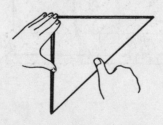

5 Make cuts in one side of the triangle about 2cm apart. Be very careful not to cut through to the opposite sides. Turn the paper around and make cuts in between the ones you have already made. Again, make sure you don't cut all the way through to the opposite sides.

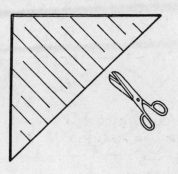

6 Carefully unfold the paper, little by little, until it is completely unfolded.

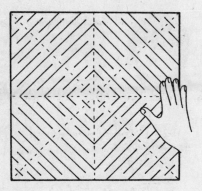

7 Gather together the corners and carefully lift them up, so as not to tear the paper, to make your . . .

8 paper net.

For a colourful mobile or hanging decoration for your room, try using the colour comic pages of a newspaper. When made much smaller the paper net will make an ideal decoration to hang on the Christmas tree.

Table mat

This is a very simple design to make, and as you open it out for display, it will bring plenty of oohs and ahs from your friends.

You will need: *small square made from a page of newspaper*
scissors

Before you start, fold the small square as far as step 4 of the paper net on pages 144–6.

1 Cut away the shaded parts shown in the diagram.

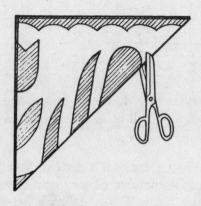

2 Carefully unfold the paper to make . . .

3 your table mat.

4 These are just a few of the many different designs that you can make. Remember never to cut large areas out of the middle, as this will weaken your finished design.

A row of figures

When we were very young we learned how to cut a row of figures from a folded sheet of newspaper. This is still the most popular of all the paper tearing effects with any audience. Recently we saw it being performed by a busker, during a Punch and Judy festival held in Covent Garden, London.

You will need: *sheet of newspaper*
felt-tip pen
scissors

1 Place the sheet of newspaper flat on a table and fold it in half from right to left along its middle fold.

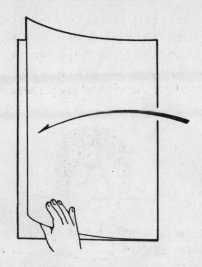

2 Fold the bottom edges up to meet the top edges. Press the newspaper flat and unfold it.

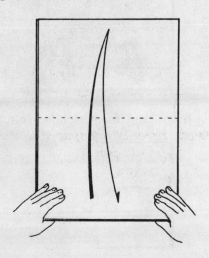

3 Cut along the fold-line to make two rectangles.

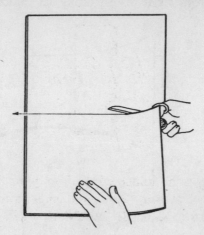

4 Taking one rectangle, fold it in half from right to left.

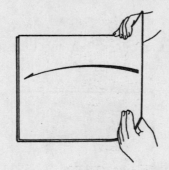

5 Fold it in half again from right to left.

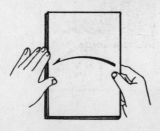

6 Press the paper flat with your thumb.

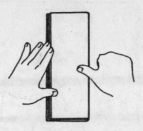

7 Starting at the folded edge, draw your figure with the felt-tip pen. Cut away the shaded parts (around the outline of your figure). Carefully unfold the paper, little by little to make . . .

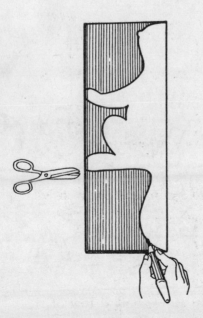

8 a row of beavers. Or a row of . . .

9 dancing girls. How about a row of . . .

Of course these are only a few of the many figures you can make. When drawing out your figure, always start so that the middle of your figure will come on the folded edge. Otherwise when you cut and open out the paper you will have two half-figures at each end. Also be careful, when you cut out your figure, that you do not completely

157

cut through the folded edges, because if you do, when you open out the paper you will have a lot of single figures. Always leave parts of the folded edges intact.

Anchor and ship's wheel

When you are cutting out this design, you could tell a story about the Captain of an old-time sailing ship. For example, you could tell how the Captain lost the anchor and ship's wheel of his sailing boat during a storm at sea. To save his boat and crew, the Captain took a sheet of newspaper and pair of scissors, and first cut out the anchor, which then became the ship's wheel.

You will need: *large square made from a sheet of newspaper scissors*

1 Lay the square of newspaper flat on a table. Fold it in half from left to right.

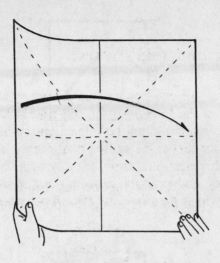

2 Fold it in half from bottom to top.

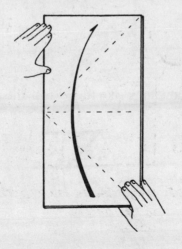

3 Fold the bottom right-hand corner up to meet the top left-hand corners to make a . . .

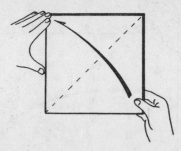

4 triangle. Fold over the top left-hand corners of the triangle so that they lie along the opposite sloping side.

5 It should now look like this. Press the paper flat with your thumbs.

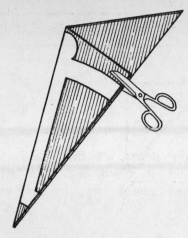

6 Cut away the shaded parts.

7 Unfold only the middle fold to make the anchor.

8 Completely unfold the anchor to make an old-fashioned ship's steering wheel.

Origami

Origami, or the art of folding paper, was first practised in Japan, and it is a very old art. We have taken a few traditional folds and adapted them so they are easy to make with newspaper.

Banger

You will need: *page of newspaper*

1 Fold the page of newspaper in half from right to left.

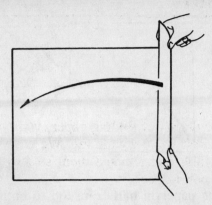

2 Fold the bottom edges up to meet the top edges. Press the paper flat.

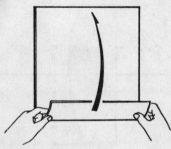

3 Completely unfold the paper.

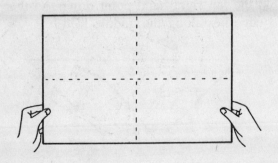

4 Fold the four corners in to meet the long fold-line.

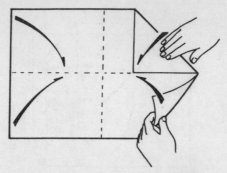

5 Fold the paper in half from top to bottom.

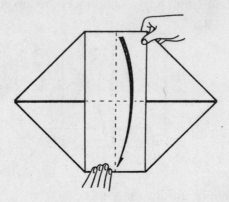

6 Fold the top right-hand point down, so that the top folded edge lies along the middle fold-line.

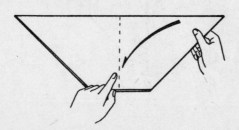

7 Fold the top left-hand point down in the same way.

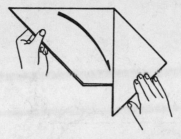

8 Fold the paper in half backwards along the middle fold-line.

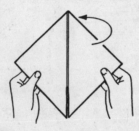

9 Hold the bottom points between your thumb and forefinger.

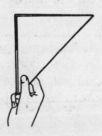

10 Swing your arm downwards very hard and the inside pocket will pop out giving a very loud bang!

To make the banger work again, just push the inside pocket back in.

Slippers

When you enter a Japanese home, you have to remove your outside shoes and put on a pair of slippers. Here is a quick and easy way to make a pair of slippers, ready for when you pay a visit.

You will need: *two sheets of newspaper*
sticky tape

1 Take one sheet of newspaper and leave it folded in half along its middle fold. With the folded edge on your right-hand side, fold the top edges down to meet the bottom edges. Press the paper flat and unfold it again.

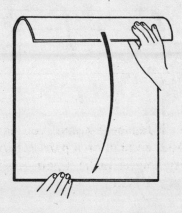

2 Fold the top edges down to a point one-third of the distance to the middle fold-line.

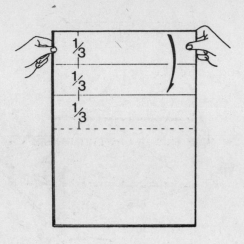

3 Fold them over again, so that they touch the middle fold-line.

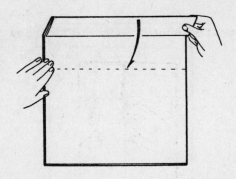

4 Your newspaper should now look like this. Turn the paper over from side to side.

5 Fold the right side in one-third of the way.

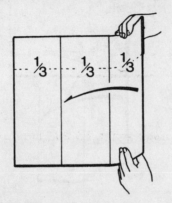

6 Put your forefinger underneath the flap and . . .

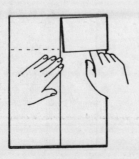

7 squash the flap outwards a little.

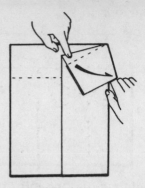

8 Fold the left side in.

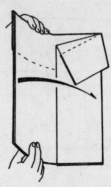

9 As before, put your forefinger underneath the flap and . . .

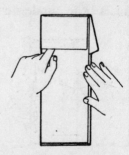

10 squash it outwards a little.

11 Fold up the bottom edges and . . .

12 tuck them, just a little, underneath the top flap.

13 Fasten down the top flap and side with sticky tape (to prevent the slipper from falling apart when you wear it).

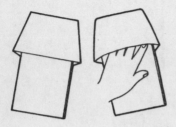

14 Turn the paper over to make your slipper.

Now fold the other sheet of newspaper in exactly the same way, to make yourself a pair of slippers.

172

Japanese paper hat

On children's day, 5 May, all Japanese children fold a paper hat. So why don't we fold this hat together?

You will need: *large square made from a sheet of newspaper*

1 Place the square on a table with a corner facing you so that it looks like a diamond. Fold up the bottom corner to touch the middle of the square.

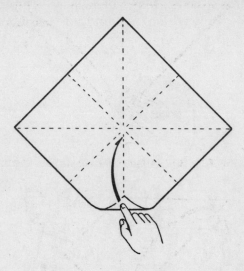

2 Fold the top corner down along the middle fold-line.

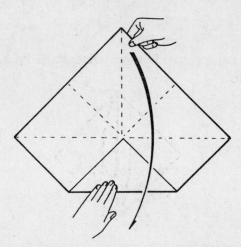

3 Bring the top right corner down, so that the top folded edge lies along the middle fold-line.

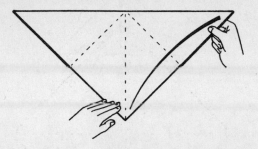

4 Fold the top left corner down in the same way.

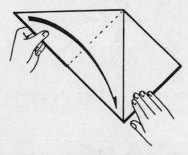

5 Fold the top two bottom points back up to meet the top point.

6 Nearly there. . . .

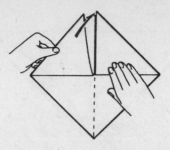

7 Now fold one of the top points out from the middle.

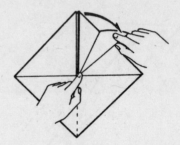

8 Fold the other top point in the same way. Turn the paper over from side to side.

9 Fold up the bottom corner to meet the middle. Turn the paper over from side to side.

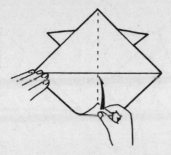

10 Fold up the bottom edge to meet the middle fold-line. In doing so, let . . .

11 the corner from underneath flick up.

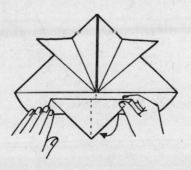

12 Fold the bottom edge up and along the middle fold-line, so making . . .

13 your hat.

Why not make one for a friend too?

Wastepaper basket

This is a very handy item to make and it is especially useful when you are cutting paper.

You will need: *sheet of newspaper*

1 Leave the sheet of newspaper folded in half along its middle fold. With the folded edge on your right-hand side, fold up the bottom edges to meet the top edges. Press the paper flat and unfold.

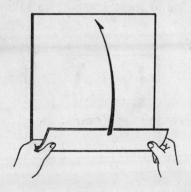

2 Fold up the bottom edges to meet the middle fold-line.

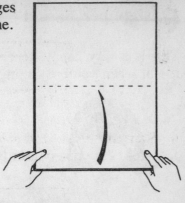

3 Fold down the top edges to meet the middle fold-line.

4 Turn the paper over from side to side. Fold down the top folded edge to meet the bottom folded edge.

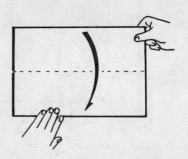

5 Fold the paper in half from right to left.

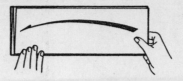

6 Stand the right-hand side upright, along the middle fold-line. Put your fingers between the layers of paper.

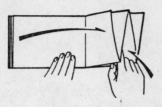

7 Start to open out the layers and with your other hand . . .

8 squash the paper down flat into this shape. Turn the paper over from side to side.

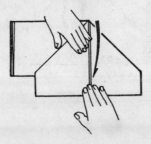

9 Stand the other side upright, along the middle fold-line. As before, put your fingers between the layers of paper.

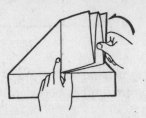

10 Start to open out the layers and with your other hand . . .

11 squash the paper down flat into this shape.

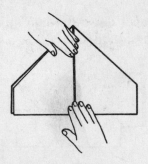

12   Fold in these two bottom corners.

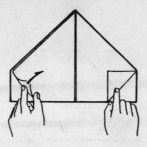

13   Reach inside the top layer of paper and very gently . . .

14   start to open out the top layer of paper into . . .

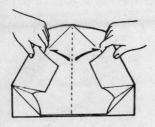

15 this shape. Press the paper flat along the sides. Turn the paper over from side to side.

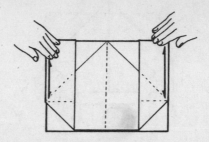

16 As before, fold in these two bottom corners.

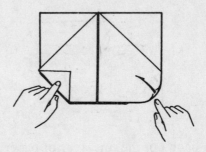

17 Reach inside the top layers of paper and very gently open them out.

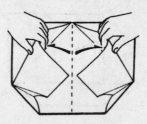

18 Press the paper flat along the sides.

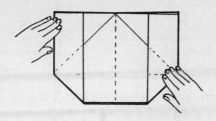

19 Fold the top layer of the left and right sides into the middle. Turn the paper over from side to side.

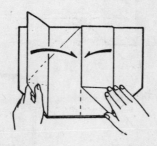

20 Fold left and right sides into the middle.

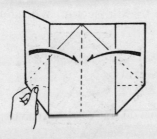

21 Press the paper flat. Turn the paper around from end to end.

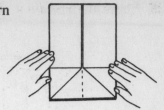

22 Fold down, as far as they will fold, the two top flaps. Fold one forwards and the other one backwards.

23 This should be your end result.

24 Hold a flap in each hand. Start to pull the flaps apart. In doing so, the middle section will start to open out.

25 Press the middle section into shape to make . . .

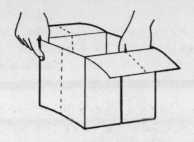

26 your wastepaper basket.

Because it is quick and inexpensive to make, the waste-paper basket and any rubbish that it contains can be thrown out as one.

Paper crown

A while ago, when we were taking part in a Japanese festival in south Germany, the grandmother of the family we were staying with showed us how to fold two party hats. This crown is one of them.

You will need: *large square made from a sheet of newspaper*

1 Place the square flat on a table and fold it in half from top to bottom.

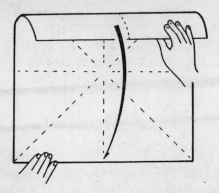

2 Fold over the right side to meet the middle fold-line.

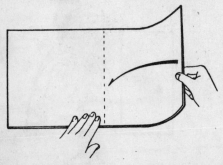

3 Fold over the left side to meet the middle fold-line.

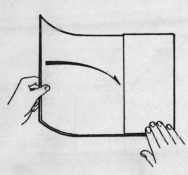

4 Lift up the right-hand side. Put your fingers inside the layers of paper.

5 Open out the layers of paper and with your free hand squash down the top into the shape of a triangular roof.

6 Do the same with the left-hand side. Lift it up. Put your fingers inside.

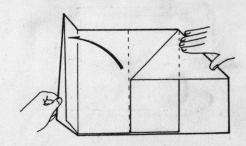

7 Open out the layers of paper and with your free hand squash down the top into the shape of a triangular roof.

8 This is the traditional origami house. Turn the paper over from side to side.

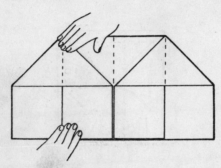

9 Fold over both sides to meet the middle fold-line.

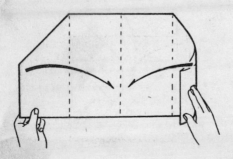

10 Fold the *top* bottom right-hand corner over to meet the middle.

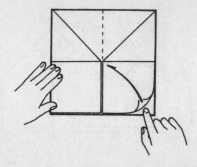

11 Fold the *top* bottom left-hand corner over to meet the middle.

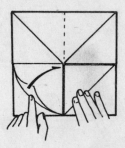

12 Fold the central bottom point up to meet the top folded edge.

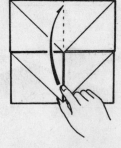

13 Press the paper flat. Turn it over from side to side.

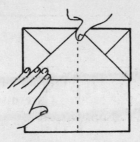

14 As before, fold over the two bottom corners to meet the middle.

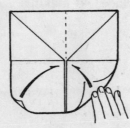

15 Fold the bottom point up to meet the top folded edge.

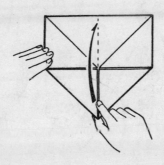

16 Press the paper flat.

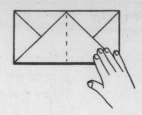

17 Put your fingers inside the crown. Carefully start to pull outwards.

18 As you do so, push the top in and shape it into place, so making your . . .

19 paper crown.

Party hat

This is the second hat we were taught how to fold when we were staying in south Germany. It is a very simple and effective way to make a super hat.

You will need: *large square made from a sheet of newspaper*

1 Place the square on a table with a corner facing you so that it looks like a diamond. Fold up the bottom corner to meet the top corner.

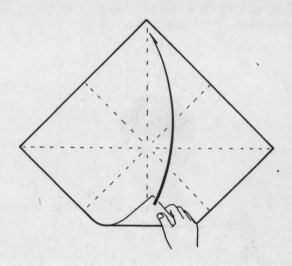

2 Fold over the left-hand side one-third of the way across the triangle.

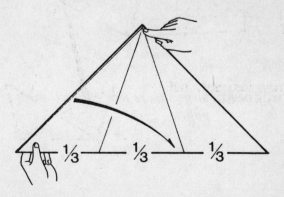

3 Fold over the right-hand side so that it lies on top.

4 Fold up the bottom points as shown.

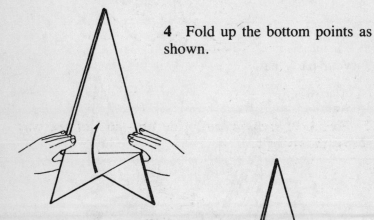

5 Press the paper flat.

6 Put your fingers between the two bottom layers and open the paper out to make . . .

7 your party hat.

The captain's hat story

To go along with the folding of this traditional paper hat, a very good friend of ours, Lillian Oppenheimer, from New York City, tells a story of a boy and how his hat becomes first a boat and then the captain's shirt. Read on to find out what happens!

You will need: *sheet of newspaper*

1 Leave the sheet of newspaper folded in half along its middle fold. With the folded edge along the top . . .

2 fold the newspaper in half from right to left. Press the paper flat.

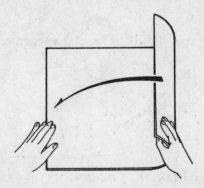

3 Unfold the paper.

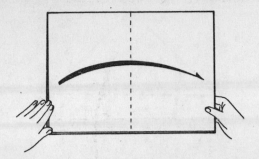

4 Fold down the top right-hand corner to meet the middle fold-line.

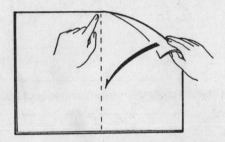

5 Fold down the top left-hand corner to meet the middle fold-line.

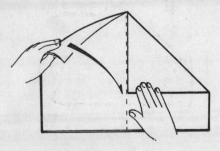

6 Fold up one single layer of paper, from the bottom up as far as it will go.

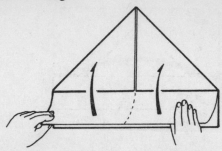

7 Press the paper flat. Turn it over from side to side.

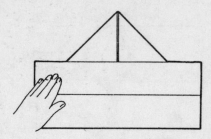

8 Fold up this single layer of paper as far as it will go.

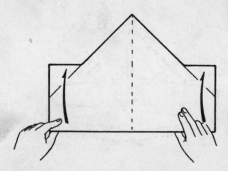

9 Press the paper flat. From the inside open out the paper a little, so making . . .

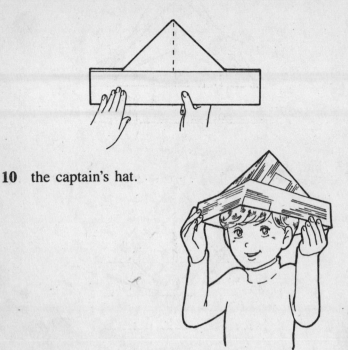

10 the captain's hat.

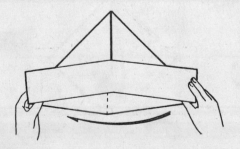

11 Hold the hat in both hands and start to . . .

12 collapse it . . .

13 into this shape.

14 Fold up the top bottom point.

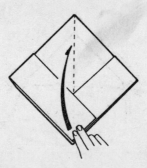

15 Press the paper flat, so making . . .

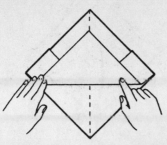

16 the fireman's hat.

17 Press the paper flat and turn it over from side to side.

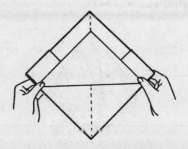

18 Fold up this bottom point.

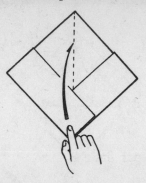

19 Hold the front and back of the hat. Carefully open out, and the hat will . . .

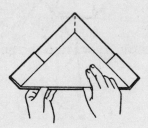

20 again collapse, to make . . .

21 the explorer's hat.

22 Press the paper flat.

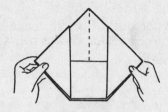

23 Fold up the top layer from the bottom of the hat.

24 Press the paper flat, and turn it over from side to side.

25 Fold up this bottom layer.

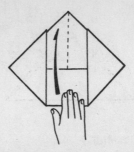

26 Open the paper out a little to make . . .

27 the pirate's hat.

28 Pinch the two side points and . . .

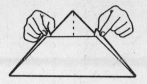

29 pull them apart to make the traditional newspaper boat.

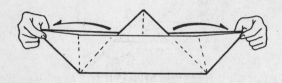

30 Now you begin to tell the story. There is a storm at sea.

31 In the storm the boat loses its stern. (*You tear one corner off.*)

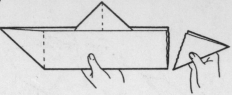

32 It also loses its bow. (*You tear the other corner off.*)

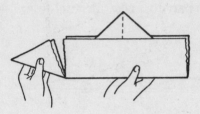

33 Last of all it loses the bridge. (*You tear the point off.*)

34 Now there is . . . (*Start to unfold what is left.*)

35 nothing left but the . . . (*Put your head through the hole.*)

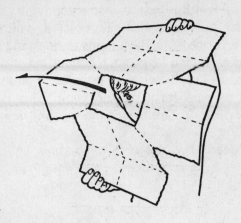

36 captain's shirt!

Troublewit

We both feel that it is best to keep a good thing until last. Maybe after you have made Troublewit, you will also think that it is one of the best items to be found in *Newspaper Magic*. Not too long ago, a famous magician, David Devant, made Troublewit very popular. You might also have seen us perform it on television. This is a much simpler version of Troublewit made from newspaper.

You will need: *two sheets of newspaper*
sticky tape

To prepare your paper, lay together the two sheets edge to edge. Fasten them together with sticky tape.

1 Carefully fold both sides to the middle.

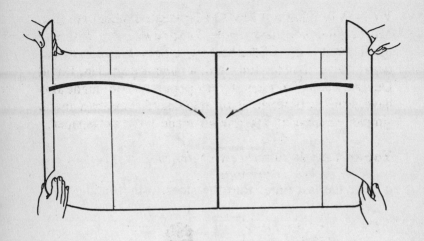

2 Again fold the sides to the middle.

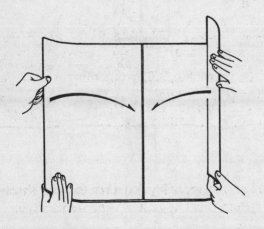

213

3 Once again, fold the sides to the middle.

4 For the last time, fold the sides to the middle.

5 Press the paper flat with your thumbs.

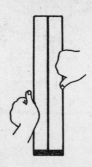

6 Open out the paper completely.

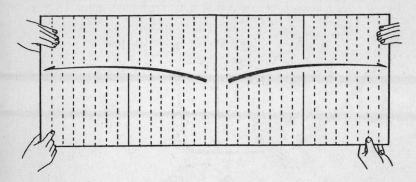

7 From one end, start to pleat the paper forwards and backwards along the fold lines, so making one long folded strip of paper, rather like a concertina. You may have to reverse some of the fold-lines.

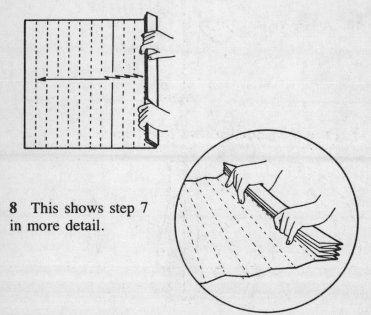

8 This shows step 7 in more detail.

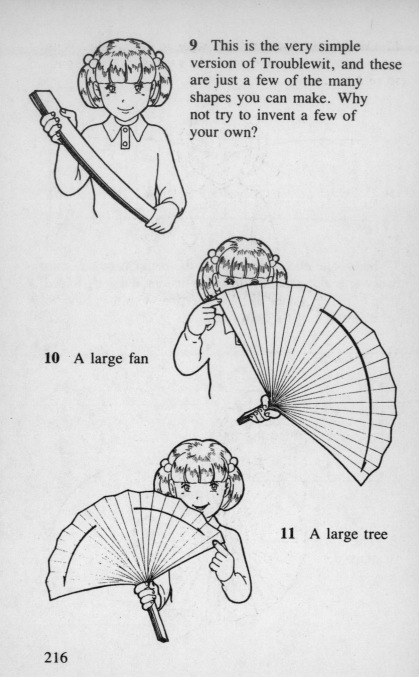

9 This is the very simple version of Troublewit, and these are just a few of the many shapes you can make. Why not try to invent a few of your own?

10 A large fan

11 A large tree

216

12 With one hand, hold the paper in the middle. With your other hand hold together the top layer of each end, so making . . .

13 A rosette

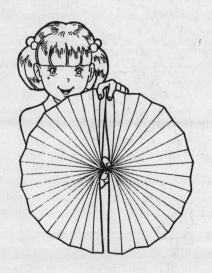

14 A punk

15 A church window

16 Fold back and hold together
the top and bottom layers
of one end to make . . .

17 A lollipop

18 The sun

19 A boat or tray

20 The End

We do hope that you have had a lot of fun and enjoyment with *Newspaper Magic*.

ACTIVITY BOOKS

If you enjoy making and doing fun things, perhaps you ought to try some of our exciting activity books. They are available in bookshops or they can be ordered directly from us. Just complete the form below and enclose the right amount of money and the books will be sent to you at home.

☐ THINGS TO MAKE IN THE HOLIDAYS	Steve and Megumi Biddle	£1.99
☐ CRAZY COOKING	Juliet Bawden	£2.25
☐ CRAZY PUPPETS	Delphine Evans	£1.95
☐ THINGS TO MAKE FOR CHRISTMAS	Eric Kenneway	£1.95
☐ THE PAPER JUNGLE	Satoshi Kitamura	£2.75
☐ SPRING CLEAN YOUR PLANET	Ralph Levinson	£1.75
☐ HOW TO MAKE SQUARE EGGS	Paul Temple and Ralph Levinson	£1.50
☐ COACHING TIPS FROM THE STARS: SOCCER	David Scott	£1.99
☐ FREAKY FASHIONS	Caroline Archer	£1.95

If you would like to order books, please send this form, and the money due to:
ARROW BOOKS, BOOKSERVICE BY POST, PO BOX 29, DOUGLAS, ISLE OF MAN, BRITISH ISLES. Please enclose a cheque or postal order made out to Arrow Books Ltd for the amount due including 22p per book for postage and packing both for orders within the UK and for overseas orders.

NAME ....

ADDRESS ....

....

Please print clearly.

Whilst every effort is made to keep prices low it is sometimes necessary to increase cover prices at short notice. Arrow Books reserve the right to show new retail prices on covers which may differ from those previously advertised in the text or elsewhere.

BEAVER BESTSELLERS

You'll find books for everyone to enjoy from Beaver's bestselling range—there are hilarious joke books, gripping reads, wonderful stories, exciting poems and fun activity books. They are available in bookshops or they can be ordered directly from us. Just complete the form below and send the right amount of money and the books will be sent to you at home.

☐ THE ADVENTURES OF KING ROLLO	David McKee	£2.50
☐ MR PINK-WHISTLE STORIES	Enid Blyton	£1.95
☐ FOLK OF THE FARAWAY TREE	Enid Blyton	£1.99
☐ REDWALL	Brian Jacques	£2.95
☐ STRANGERS IN THE HOUSE	Joan Lingard	£1.95
☐ THE RAM OF SWEETRIVER	Colin Dann	£2.50
☐ BAD BOYES	Jim and Duncan Eldridge	£1.95
☐ ANIMAL VERSE	Raymond Wilson	£1.99
☐ A JUMBLE OF JUNGLY JOKES	John Hegarty	£1.50
☐ THE RETURN OF THE ELEPHANT JOKE BOOK	Katie Wales	£1.50
☐ THE REVENGE OF THE BRAIN SHARPENERS	Philip Curtis	£1.50
☐ THE RUNAWAYS	Ruth Thomas	£1.99
☐ EAST OF MIDNIGHT	Tanith Lee	£1.99
☐ THE BARLEY SUGAR GHOST	Hazel Townson	£1.50
☐ CRAZY COOKING	Juliet Bawden	£2.25

If you would like to order books, please send this form, and the money due to:
ARROW BOOKS, BOOKSERVICE BY POST, PO BOX 29, DOUGLAS, ISLE OF MAN, BRITISH ISLES. Please enclose a cheque or postal order made out to Arrow Books Ltd for the amount due including 22p per book for postage and packing both for orders within the UK and for overseas orders.

NAME ....

ADDRESS ....

....
Please print clearly.

Whilst every effort is made to keep prices low it is sometimes necessary to increase cover prices at short notice. Arrow Books reserve the right to show new retail prices on covers which may differ from those previously advertised in the text or elsewhere.

ENID BLYTON

If you are an eager Beaver reader, perhaps you ought to try some of our exciting Enid Blyton titles. They are available in bookshops or they can be ordered directly from us. Just complete the form below, enclose the right amount of money and the books will be sent to you at home.

☐ THE CHILDREN OF CHERRY-TREE FARM	£1.99
☐ THE CHILDREN OF WILLOW FARM	£1.99
☐ NAUGHTY AMELIA JANE	£1.50
☐ AMELIA JANE AGAIN	£1.50
☐ THE BIRTHDAY KITTEN	£1.50
☐ THE VERY BIG SECRET	£1.50
☐ THE ADVENTUROUS FOUR	£1.50
☐ THE ADVENTUROUS FOUR AGAIN	£1.50
☐ THE NAUGHTIEST GIRL IS A MONITOR	£1.95
☐ THE NAUGHTIEST GIRL IN THE SCHOOL	£1.95
☐ THE ENCHANTED WOOD	£1.99
☐ THE WISHING-CHAIR AGAIN	£1.99
☐ HURRAH FOR THE CIRCUS	£1.75

If you would like to order books, please send this form, and the money due to:
ARROW BOOKS, BOOKSERVICE BY POST, PO BOX 29, DOUGLAS, ISLE OF MAN, BRITISH ISLES. Please enclose a cheque or postal order made out to Arrow Books Ltd for the amount due including 22p per book for postage and packing both for orders within the UK and for overseas orders.

NAME ....

ADDRESS ....

....

Please print clearly.

Whilst every effort is made to keep prices low it is sometimes necessary to increase cover prices at short notice. Arrow Books reserve the right to show new retail prices on covers which may differ from those previously advertised in the text or elsewhere.

JOKE BOOKS

Have you heard about all the hilarious joke books published by Beaver? They are available in bookshops or they can be ordered directly from us. Just complete the form below and enclose the right amount of money and the books will be sent to you at home.

☐ THE SMELLY SOCKS JOKE BOOK	Susan Abbott	£1.95
☐ THE VAMPIRE JOKE BOOK	Peter Eldin	£1.50
☐ THE WOBBLY JELLY JOKE BOOK	Jim Eldridge	£1.50
☐ A JUMBLE OF JUNGLY JOKES	John Hegarty	£1.50
☐ NOT THE ELEPHANT JOKE BOOK	John Hegarty	£1.50
☐ THE CRAZY CRAZY JOKE BAG	Janet Rogers	£1.95
☐ THE CRAZIEST JOKE BOOK EVER	Janet Rogers	£1.50
☐ THE ELEPHANT JOKE BOOK	Katie Wales	£1.00
☐ THE RETURN OF THE ELEPHANT JOKE BOOK	Katie Wales	£1.50
☐ JOKES FROM OUTER SPACE	Katie Wales	£1.25
☐ SANTA'S CHRISTMAS JOKE BOOK	Katie Wales	£1.50

If you would like to order books, please send this form, and the money due to:
ARROW BOOKS, BOOKSERVICE BY POST, PO BOX 29, DOUGLAS, ISLE OF MAN, BRITISH ISLES. Please enclose a cheque or postal order made out to Arrow Books Ltd for the amount due including 22p per book for postage and packing both for orders within the UK and for overseas orders.

NAME . . . .

ADDRESS . . . .

. . . .

Please print clearly.

Whilst every effort is made to keep prices low it is sometimes necessary to increase cover prices at short notice. Arrow Books reserve the right to show new retail prices on covers which may differ from those previously advertised in the text or elsewhere.